PREPARE TO FAIL

PLAN TO SUCCEED

Tones A Chord

Introduction:

This will <u>not</u> make you successful. It will <u>not</u> cause you to fail. If you prepare for the common causes of failure, you have a better chance of succeeding. Management by exception happens when the regular activities have been addressed and are working. Those situations that can't be planned for happen in every business. When these happen management can address these without worrying about the regular activities functioning. Each chapter addresses a point that can, individually, doom an enterprise. Your goal is to limit each so that you are prepared to overcome difficulties before they happen. This can be due to forces not under your control or simply due to an oversight that could have been handled up front.

More businesses fail for lack of planning than for lack of product. Aptitude (planning), Attitude, and product knowledge are necessary for success, in that order. This is true even as Attitude is 98% of success. The best attitude, without planning and preparation, has lost many a ball game.

Following are thirty-two steps to overcome business challenges…that may cause you to fail.

When you realize you are not in charge you will seek the help you need to succeed.

"I want you to work for me. I don't want to pay you enough to feed your family, pay your mortgage, or send your children to school. Insurance premiums will have to come out of your pocket. I want you to work for me from three to five years without an income. Meanwhile, I'll pay you enough to pay for my products and taxes. I'll even kick in a little to pay for your employees. I expect you to live off a business loan and pay interest during that time."

Who am I? Why, "I'm your customer when you start a new business!"

This is what you face in starting a business! The customer is concerned about: A) Value of your product B) the service you are able to provide and C) the actual cost of your product.

The cost of your product includes quality, warranty, and service. Who is responsible for adjustments, repairs, and replacements covered by the warranty? Are you prepared to do this or do you have to send the products to the manufacturer? How fast is service? Is the service done right and at a reasonable price?

- Quality- Are you producing a product? What is the quality?
  Are you promoting a supplier's product? What is the quality?
- Warranty- What warranty are you offering? Repair, replacement, local service, factory service, what is to be covered, for how long?
- Service- Do you have the skills to do regular repairs and service? What is the cost to the customer?

You cannot control the expectations of your customer. In order to stay in business, you must strive to understand those expectations and meet those expectations. You also must acknowledge when you <u>cannot</u> meet those expectations and be willing to walk away from a sale. PLAN TO SUCCEED!

"Unless a person has failed, that person has never known success" The key here is that the only way to know if you have stretched the most is when you stretch so much you fail. Then you know your limits! Learn the ways you can fail and your limits will be higher! Know the point of failure and reach to the point below.

Success comes when failure is overcome. Those who see failure as a temporary setback and are able to work through failure will succeed. PLAN TO SUCCEED!

Table of Contents:

Chapter 1 Employees

Chapter 2 Benefits

Chapter 3 Bricks and Mortar

Chapter 4 Product

Chapter 5 Inventory

Chapter 6 Insurance

Chapter 7 Taxes

Chapter 8 Economy

Chapter 9 Statutes/Laws

Chapter 10 Unions

Chapter 11 Legal

Chapter 12 Business Type

Chapter 13 Utilities

Chapter 14 Service

Chapter 15 Samples

Chapter 16 Advertising

Chapter 17 Business Plan

Chapter 18 Product Sources

Chapter 19 Banking

Chapter 20 Customers

Chapter 21 Sales

Chapter 22 Location

Chapter 23 Logo

Chapter 24 Signage

Chapter 25 Trademark

Chapter 26 New/Existing

Chapter 27 Mentor

Chapter 28 social media

Chapter 29 Tools

Chapter 30 Office Supplies

Chapter 31 Technology

Chapter 32 Ethics

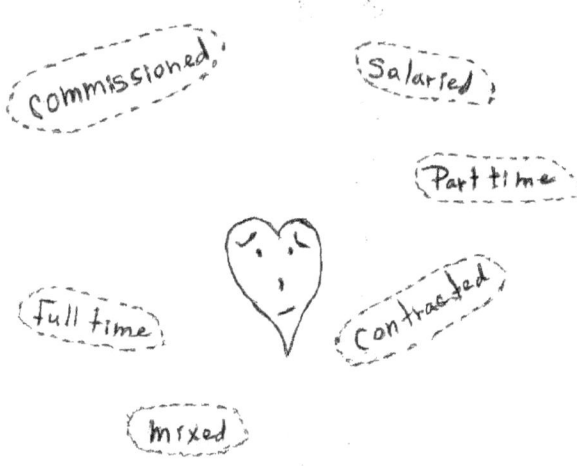

Chapter 1   Employees

Hire employees not needed. Hire employees not able to perform. Hire employees who are dishonest or unethical. Hire employees who are not personable and customer focused. Hire employees who do not have a work ethic. You PREPARE TO FAIL!   If you are one of "those employees" you PREPARE TO FAIL!

In order to run the business, how much can you do yourself? Do you need employees? What do you need done that you can not do yourself? Considering the workload, which necessary tasks are you not able to do?

For those employees you absolutely need:

How are they paid?

- Commission: a percentage of sales. This can be personal sales or production sales (in which the producer depends on someone doing personal sales in order to earn their commission). Commissions can vary anywhere from 5% to 40%. Setting the commission level is an art.
- It depends on your overhead, cost of the product, employee benefits, cost to service loans, and personal profit. What is the employee

required to do to earn the commission? Are in-store sales

the goal? Is the employee to be an outside salesperson (Contacting prospective customers, getting orders, fulfilling orders, delivering

orders, etc.)? The commission should adequately reimburse the

employee for the effort expended. It should also allow for profit to

pay their business expenses. PLAN TO SUCCEED!

- Salary: a set amount per hour. Your cost per hour will include
- payroll, social security payments, Medicare payments, a set amount
- for support (store expenses, bookkeeping, insurance, etc.) When considering the wage scale consider the possibility of a forty-hour week. What is the possibility of overtime? Can the business income afford the salary (keeping in mind the employer's taxes)?

Is the employee earning the salary? Is there an ability for the employee to progress with effort? The cost of an employee's salary and benefits should reflect the employee's value to the business. Planning to survive on today's minimum wages, PREPARE TO SUCCEED!

- A legislative action increasing the minimum wage (either Federal or State) when you do not have the profits to bear the cost requires you to reduce the number of hours worked, reduce the number of employees, or increase the income from increased business, either volume or increased product prices. PLAN TO SUCCEED!

- Salary plus commission: Minimum salary keeps the risk lower and gives the employee an income while learning the job, and commission allows the employee to earn more based on performance.

  This allows the company to pay as the company's sales rise and fall, while staying in business. It also gives an incentive for the employee to want the business to be successful. PLAN TO SUCCEED!

- Salary plus bonus: This gives the employee a fair wage and rewards the employee for helping the business succeed. A bonus can be in the form of cash, payment to a medical savings account, payment to a retirement account, or reducing the premium of health insurance. Normally the bonus is allocated at the end of the year and is based on profits. There is a danger of the employee becoming used to the bonus and demanding the bonus in a year when profits do not allow it. ALWAYS let them know the profits and how they are given or not given. PLAN TO SUCCEED!

- Commission plus bonus: This has the effect of allowing the employee to earn based on production while getting a bonus based on the performance of the business.

The method of payment can vary by employee. It is an agreement between the employer and the employee.

Paying an employee (or yourself) more than production allows will lead to failure. This area is the biggest cost of any business.

Keep in mind that each employee (Including the owner and managers) must EARN the cost of employment. For every dollar of "take home" pay, the employee must produce a minimum of two dollars of income

to pay the bills associated with the employment (Social Security, Medicare, income taxes and business overhead). Each employee must be employed to <u>work</u>. Having a job just to have an income will not allow the business to pay the bills efficiently.

> Example: An employee is paid $15.00 per hour. That's your initial cost for the hour worked. Social security and Medicare payments are deducted from that. Income tax is deducted from that. Take home pay is reduced for the employee. In addition to paying the $15.00 per hour you will match the

> social security payments, factor in a portion of business expenses needed to keep the doors open and maintain the job for the employee, and factor the business profit. Think of Mortgage/rent, utilities, office staff, office supplies, advertising, over-time, insurance, paid vacations, paid sick

leave time and any retirement plan, (take annual costs divided by person-hours worked).

Your cost to maintain that employee can easily exceed $30.00 per hour.

BEGIN: lean

Keep employment to the minimum needed to keep the business running. Commissions are a good way to keep expenses in line with income. Do what you can do yourself as much as possible. PLAN to SUCCEED!

It has been estimated that a business must have $250,000 of additional Gross sales in order to support one additional salaried employee. That estimate should allow the employee $25,000 of take-home pay. The other way to look at it is, the employee must produce $250,000 of Gross sales to receive $25,000 income. Four employees (including you) would require gross sales of one million a year.

Grow your skills to be knowledgeable in the business. Know your costs. Keep the costs down. Cut waste and excesses. A simple act of replacing tools can be very costly.

UPS cut expenses dramatically by the "Right Turn". Think about it! Thousands of gallons of fuel are wasted at stop lights. The ability to turn right, after stop, reduces the time stopped and reduces the fuel wasted. It's a small adjustment, planning the routes to increase right turns, that makes a tremendous savings in the bottom line. Many times, it is the small adjustments that make a successful business.

Jerry Lewis studied the camera person, the make-up people, all those behind the scenes, and became a very successful director in addition to his acting skills. Knowing each part of the business is necessary for real success.

What utilities, rent, travel, time, etc. costs can you optimize. Keep in mind that adequate income and benefits can work both ways. Employees can be more productive. On the other hand, depending on the benefits without a work ethic and productivity makes benefits a drain on the business. PLAN to SUCCEED.

The employee is the engine that makes a business grow. I walked into a large chain store several times to shop. The employees stood around talking to each other or wandering around checking inventory. Not once did an employee make eye contact, smile and ask to help me find what I needed. I eventually found what I went in for but soon went to a competitor who saved me valuable time by helping me get what I needed quickly. Time is money! A good employee is customer oriented and focuses on the customer! A good employee grows your business and earns the cost of keeping that employee.

An employee with a bad attitude or a sour personality can drive more business away than five good employees can attract. A customer of mine commented on a local grocery store. "I'll never shop on the weekends. The student employees (college students) are rude." The grocery store is fortunate she is willing to shop there on another day of the week. When you hire PLAN to SUCCEED!

Don't forget the employees behind the machine- Bookkeeping, Office administration (Phone, customer service, appointments, time charts, payroll, etc.), Sales and Service. This is the machine- production and delivery,

Good, specific job descriptions are necessary for a smooth operation. Limiting the ability of an employee to the specific job description denies the ability to fill in if necessary for another position. PLAN TO SUCCEED!

Does the employee add value to the business? There are qualities an employee must bring to the business.

Ethics is a must. Every employee must treat both the employer and the customer with honesty and respect.

Personality is a must. Every employee must have a friendly presentation toward customers and other employees.

Work ethic is a must. Each employee must strive to make the business run well and grow. PLAN TO SUCCEED!

While keeping the number of employees to a minimum, helping you pay your bills and grow the business, your goal is to be able to increase the number of employees as your business grows. Keep your priorities in order. Without the business no employees are necessary. In order to grow your business, you must have motivated employees. You must pay your bills. You must serve your customers. You must have help. PLAN TO SUCCEED!

In order to hire, train and grow employees it is important to know what an employee needs and what an employee must add to the business for the business to be successful. Are you willing to put forth more effort than you are paid for? Are you willing to go beyond the requirement of your job without demanding more compensation? How will you go the extra mile to help your employer succeed? Are you the type of employee that will keep your employer in business so you can have a job in the future? Are you the employee you will need to succeed? PLAN TO SUCCEED!

Don't forget the primary employee…YOU! Are you going to work on a salary? Are you able and willing to work only on a commission?

Can you budget your income to pay the bills, set aside savings for the lean times, and have needed cash for personal expenses? As the primary employee you are responsible to yourself and family to pay bills on time, pay down your debt, pay employees, and put food on the table. Working on a salary puts food on the table even when bills are paid by borrowed money.

Receiving a commission requires paying bills and loans first and living on the rest.

If you are able to work on commission you have a better chance of success. You are required to take care of customers and those depending on you first. That   leads to a more successful relationship. PLAN TO SUCCEED!

An employer hired relatives to give them an income. He had more employees than the income from the business could afford. The business did not allow for them to add productivity. In the end the business failed and was lost. Had he simply helped their income with profits from the business the business would have had a better chance to succeed? Watch your overhead! PLAN TO SUCCEED!

Chapter 2   Benefits

Don't worry about taxes and benefits. They will take care of themselves! Sales will cover these expenses. You PREPARE TO FAIL!

Required Benefits: Social Security, Medicare, Liability insurance, fair wage, office support, and training.

Other benefits: Health Insurance, Retirement package, paid leave time, production bonuses, gifts, education support, all add up.

Benefits can change over time. They MUST be in writing. The benefits package (or lack thereof) must be explained to the employee at initial training and a copy of understanding must be signed by the employee.

Kathy was allowed to enter a group health insurance plan sponsored by her employer. Kathy paid the premiums and chose the benefits. She chose not to have maternity health insurance as she was not married. Within a year Kathy was pregnant and filed a claim for maternity coverage. Although she was at risk to becoming pregnant, she felt she did not need the coverage. A signed understanding agreement would help remind her of the choice! Communication helps prevent the provider from being upset at the insurance company for not covering a service.

Employee health insurance premiums are generally paid for by both the employer and the employee. The employer may pay for the employee cost and the employee pays for the family coverage. The employer may be wholly or partially "self-insured". This means that the employer acts as an insurance company and pays the health care bills. When the employees strive to stay healthy an employer may bonus savings of the estimated costs to the employees at the end of the year.

Retirement benefits may run from individual plans to employer sponsored plans. Contributions may be entirely by the employer, or the employee or a combination of both.

Taxes must be paid on time! Governments do NOT have a sense of humor for delayed taxes. Like any other employee they need to be paid promptly. Income taxes, Social Security, Medicare, Sales taxes, Property taxes, intangibles taxes, and business development district taxes, all must be paid.

After moving across town to a new business location the city dragged their feet approving a sign permit. This caused lost sales and increased debt to keep the business going. Soon after the move a letter came from the city requiring immediate payment of several hundred dollars for the Business development district tax with the caveat that an unpaid tax would incur a visit from the attorney. When moving, the process of getting a sign permit and the need for the special tax were not known. This lack of knowledge was expensive and almost ended the business. It took five years to recover from the unexpected losses. PLAN TO SUCCEED

Chapter 3   Bricks and Mortar

You wait until the business is going to find a location and figure the cost of the location. You "PREPARE TO FAIL"

Purchase a building: Think Mortgage! Borrow the money at 8% interest and add the annual cost of payments to the hourly production needed. When an owned building is not mortgaged the same formula applies. The building must be paid so repairs, upgrades, replacement can be handled. Is the loan a fixed loan or an adjustable loan? If an adjustable loan has a limit to the adjustment (e.g., 2% per year maximum increase) and the loan can be paid off in the worst-case scenario (the interest rate reached 10% by the time the loan is paid off), an adjustable loan may be a good choice. If a fixed interest loan is available that incurs similar interest rates over the expected loan period, then it may be better to have a fixed interest loan that may actually have a lower interest rate at the end of the term and be lower should you exceed your planned pay off date.

Lease a building: The rent will cover the payments of the landlord plus his upkeep costs taxes and profit. If you assume a "triple net" lease you will pay insurance and upkeep for the landlord in addition to the rent. What will cause the rent to increase? Do property taxes go up regularly? Are they scheduled to go up? Whether the landlord or you pay these taxes directly, you will pay them. How long a lease can you afford?

How long a lease can you agree to? A several years lease helps level the costs over time and can help you succeed. Fewer surprises here can make the difference whether you succeed or fail.

A LEASE/PURCHASE option can be a good choice. This is where the location is optimal, the building is useable and in good shape, and the seller and buyer can come to an agreement on price, interest, and payments. The Buyer agrees to purchase the facility directly from the Seller for a set price (normally asset value plus interest over the lease period), spread out over a period of years. This should be accompanied by a BUY/SELL agreement where the entire amount is paid off in the event one of the parties should die before the facility is paid off. Insuring this agreement guarantees the money is available when needed.

EXAMPLE: Joe agrees to purchase a business worth $300,000 over ten years at 4% interest. At simple interest that adds $12,000. The BUY/SELL agreement is set for $312,000 and the annual payments would be $31,200 for 10 years. The Buyer would insure the life of the seller for $312,000 and pay premiums on the policy. The Buyer would also insure his own life for $312,000. If either dies before the ten years is up the money is available to complete the purchase. The yearly payments and the amount of premiums need to be considered when determining the income needed from the business. If the interest were added annually or compounded the payments would be different.

You may be able to run your business out of your home. Independent direct sales of products from companies such as Mary Kay, Shaklee, Re Liv, Stanley, Watkins, Tupperware, and Amway work primarily from home offices. Real Estate, Insurance, Accounting and other service businesses have been successful as home-based businesses. Will your income pay the mortgage, taxes, utilities, and family expenses? PLAN TO SUCCEED!

PRODUCT

CHAPTER 4   PRODUCT

Pick a product that you like. Make it fit your lifestyle. Produce a product your friend is enthusiastic about! It all sounds good. You PREPARE TO FAIL.

A product will not be marketable because you like it or a friend likes it. It will be marketable because the consumer likes it and needs it. Pick a product that is used on a daily basis, is renewable, and can be made affordable. Pick a product that your consumer survey (yes, you need to find out what consumers response will be before starting on this venture) tells you the consumers are enthused about.

- Needed
- Wanted
- Available
- Affordable
- Marketable
- Renewable

SO! Are you going to market an existing product or are you going to bring a new product to the market?

- Why is it needed?
- Who wants it?
- How can you make it Available?
- Can you keep it affordable and cover your expense and have an income?
- What marketing will be effective to reach those who want it and can afford it?

How long will it take to get the business going once you decide to jump?

- How long to get financing?
- What is the lag time to get products available?
- What will it take to set up a store?
- How long will it take to train employees? What is the estimated cost for training?
- How are you going to pay expenses from start up to sales?
- Do you have an exit strategy to fall back on if the business doesn't go?
- How will you pay the loans, rent, etc. if the business doesn't go?   PLAN TO SUCCEED!

Needed: Is the product needed for food, shelter, clothing, or business?

Food and water are necessary for survival. Is there a way to provide these more efficiently or with better service?

Is the shelter needed and wanted? Tents are good shelter for camping, hiking and hunting. They are also used for homes in some areas. What is the need for shelter? Look outside the box!

Clothing is necessary for warmth. Clothing can be designed for all types of weather. Utility, style, and function are necessary for the consumer to purchase clothing.

A business may be to supply food, service shelter, and repair clothing.

Who provides transportation, shipping, and warehousing to get the product to market?

In the end, the consumer makes the decision if it is marketable. PLAN TO SUCCEED!

Going Business Concern- A business already established can answer all these questions for you. Often the answers will be easier and the chances for success greater. Look for a business you can learn and are able to run. Look for a business that the owner is close to retirement and needs someone to buy the business. Consider an insured buy-sell agreement. That guarantees money will be available (at a discount) should death come before the business is paid off. PLAN TO SUCCEED!

Some businesses are more profitable than others. Farming is a high risk where debt can easily bring failure. Here it is especially important to learn the particular enterprise (Land, crops, average weather, markets) and definitely have an insured buy sell agreement in place providing enough to pay off the enterprise and provide two years of operation expenses. The loss of a key person (previous owner in this situation) always causes waves in an operation, especially if this occurs early in the agreement.

Other businesses are highly profitable. These usually require long hours of work for the owner and income on commission only. Insurance sales, Real Estate Sales, Home Multi-Level Marketing sales, are some examples. These can require a minimum of three years to get established and may have limited income during the "start-up" period.

You've got to lay the foundation before the business can be built.

Laying the foundation always requires hard work and learning. Licensing may be needed; Courses may be required. These must be considered in start-up costs. PLAN TO SUCCEED!

I started a small business producing a specialty "pusher" snow shovel. The survey indicated there is a market. The shovel did not require lifting the snow. It reduced the heart rate acquired with a regular snow shovel. The back injuries were almost eliminated. The factory manufactured 1200 initial supply. Some of the simple machines did not work. Without knowing which ones worked and which ones didn't we stopped sales. Over twenty years later we still haven't resolved the situation. The initial loan was $45,000. The estimated cost so far is over $150,000 with interest. I should have set up an inspection system.

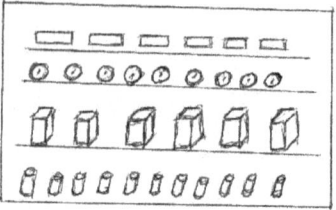

Chapter 5   Inventory

Fill the warehouse. Get ready for shipping! You PREPARE TO FAIL.

Look at pre-orders. "Order for delivery in 60 days". You see this in Music CD sales. If you can produce the product and ship it within 60 days this is a great way to start. You don't have the cost of sitting on inventory and paying interest on the money loaned for more than a few days. If the pre-order is pre-paid you don't have the cost of interest.

Jack self-published a book and had 20,000 copies printed. They didn't sell. The out-of-pocket cost should have been avoided. Had Jack started with a publish-on-demand he could have tied in with the demand on a current basis until the book "took off". If Jack had promoted the book while writing it and notified his contacts when it was finished the chances of success would have greatly improved.

The goal here is to set your prices so that you will have the money to purchase 10% more than the pre-order. This helps you transition to regular sales. If the product is well received there will be continuing orders after the initial 60 days. If the initial sales are flat you must determine whether you will be able to sell enough to continue or need to stop. In either case you have reduced your cost by not "filling the warehouse". PLAN TO SUCCEED!

Are you taxed on your inventory? Do you pay sales taxes when you receive the inventory? Do you pay sales taxes when you sell the inventory?

   What rent do you pay for the space needed for inventory? What is the difference in cost for your product by keeping a large inventory? Plan for a small inventory with a basic load. PLAN TO SUCCEED!

A basic load is calculated with two variables. What is the delay between ordering and receiving? And, how long is a product in inventory before being sold? An example would be a product that you can receive within fourteen days and you plan a thirty day turnover. Ordering half of your need every two weeks will keep inventory at a minimum, reducing your cost of the product. PLAN TO SUCCEED

In a going business inventory may already be in place. Adjustments may be   able to be made to increase profit. Keeping inventory at a level that the customer can be serviced quickly while reducing parts or products that have   little turn-over may be a small adjustment. This, over time, can yield good returns.

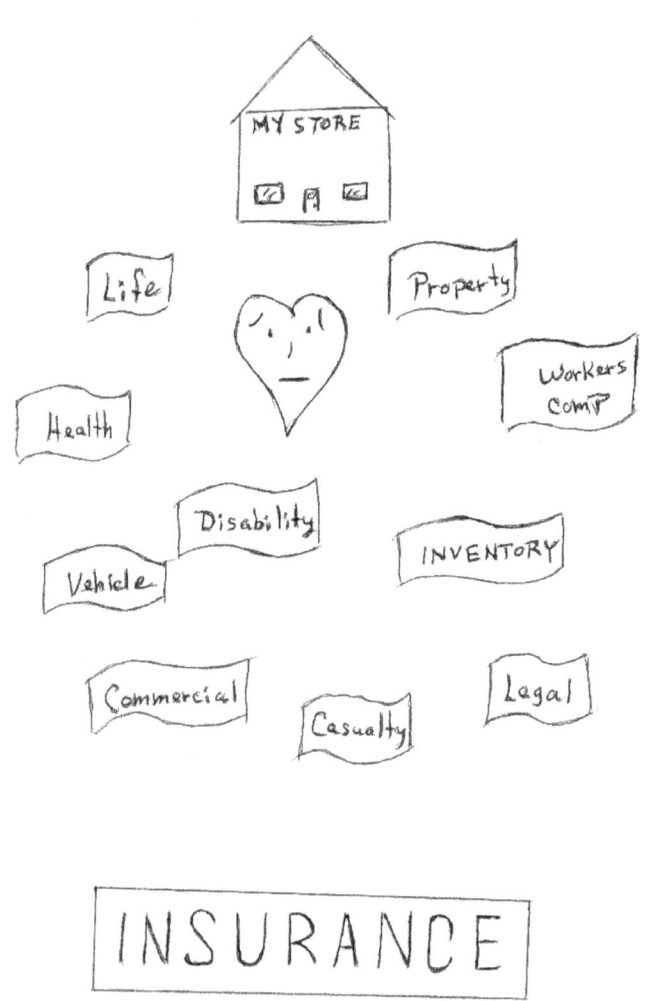

Chapter 6   Insurance

Wait on insurance until the profits come in and you can afford it. You PREPARE TO FAIL!

More good businesses are lost with the loss of the key person. The "idea person" who plans the business, knows the market, has the contacts, motivates the employees, and pays the bills is the anchor. A sudden death or disability here can cause the business to fold. Life and Disability insurance (business continuation plan) is needed at the beginning. This is the time that the key person is most insurable. A business should always be set up with an "exit" strategy.

- When the Key Person Dies
- When the Key Person becomes disabled
- When the Key Person retires

This applies to the one being trained to replace the Key Person. Financing can help transition. Leadership needs to be in place for continuation.

Health insurance, life insurance, accident insurance, and disability insurance should be available for employees. There are possibilities where an employee pays for some insurance on a payroll deduction basis and the premiums are not included in the (social security) taxable income. Specialty health insurance, long and short-term disability, and life insurance are areas an employee can be helped with.

Business continuation insurance in case of a nature event (hurricane, tornado, earthquake, and flood) that can continue paying salaries, rent/mortgage, and re-building expenses is necessary. The majority of business failures due to weather do not have this insurance

Your initial start-up loan should cover the cost of insurance for three years. PLAN TO SUCCEED!

A thriving business, developing electric cars failed when the man who had the vision, contacts, and ability to grow the business suddenly died. No one was prepared to succeed him. Contacts were lost. The vision of continuing did not survive. The business was dependent on one individual. When he "stepped out" no transition was set up for continuation. The business folded. PLAN TO SUCCEED!

Key person insurance, business interruption insurance (floods, fire, tornado, hurricane, etc.), can help recover from those events that you cannot control. Paying taxes is one you can control. PLAN TO SUCCEED!

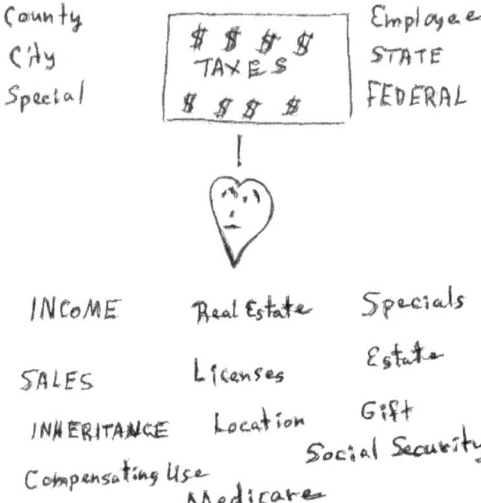

County   Employee
City   STATE
Special   FEDERAL

INCOME   Real Estate   Specials

SALES   Licenses   Estate

INHERITANCE   Location   Gift

Compensating Use   Social Security

Medicare

TAXES

Chapter 7   Taxes

Don't worry about taxes. They aren't due until profits are made! You PREPARE TO FAIL

Company taxes can come in the form of Corporate, Local, Sales, Real Estate, Income, Employment, Workers Compensation, Unemployment, and license fees.

Any or all of these are set up to allow the government entities to shut you down. You must pay to play. Plan to pay all taxes owed on time every time. They don't care if you ever make a sale. Taxes are due just because you are in business. PLAN TO SUCCEED!

We covered the cost of employees earlier. Each employee must produce enough to cover the expenses related to the employment. Each employee must produce enough to also contribute to the cost of operations and insurance needed. PLAN TO SUCCEED!

If you don't pay sales taxes to your state (where there are sales taxes) the state will take your inventory and lock your door. If you don't pay employee taxes (social security, Medicare, income taxes) the government will provide you with housing and food in a secure facility. PLAN TO SUCCEED!

There are businesses today that are headed for the graveyard. They are good businesses with a good customer base and good revenue. The owner is at or approaching retirement and no one is interested in learning the business to take it over. Many of these businesses do not need a degree. They need someone who can work hard, learn the business, have a customer service attitude, and be able to manage money and keep the bills paid. That includes taxes. The government will shut down a business faster than a creditor. They don't need to go to court. They just move in and take assets overnight. You can go to work Monday morning and find an empty establishment. Bills need to keep paid. PLAN TO SUCCEED!

Employees not on the federal radar! These can be good workers and valuable to the business. Not paying income, Social Security, and Medicare taxes will earn you a visit from the Feds. Go to the trouble for legal documentation! PLAN TO SUCCEED!

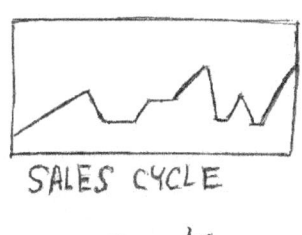

SALES CYCLE

ECONOMY

Chapter 8   Economy

Don't watch the economy. People always buy, no matter the economy! You PREPARE TO FAIL!

The housing market has its ups and downs. Foods have their ups and downs. Clothing has ups and downs. Your market will have ups and downs.

- What market cycle is conducive to marketing your product?
- How will you maintain paying expenses in the opposing market cycle?
- How do you know what cycle you are in?
- How do you know when cycles are about to change?
- What will you do to prepare for down times?

When deciding on a product find out how it does in a down market. If sales in a down market are sufficient to pay the bills and have an income then plan your business to function at that level. If more employees are needed in good times let them know the risk of being "laid off" in a down cycle to preserve the business. Sometimes the cycles are so short temporary workers can fill the void in the up cycles. A prolonged, up cycle will be more efficient with full time workers. They may help extend the good cycle when a down cycle starts. PLAN TO SUCCEED

Many businesses do half of their annual sales within six weeks. The Thanksgiving and Christmas seasons are the good cycles. The rest of the year they get the other half. If they are only open for the good seasons the sales then will not be good. People shop at stores they feel are permanent. It's the rest of the year that the businesses advertise that they are there for the customer. It's those weeks that convince the customers to shop in the up cycles. Plan for the down cycles to be there for the up cycles. PLAN TO SUCCEED!

In our business we don't have specific times when sales are better. Tracking the years two months seem better and two months are slowest. We never know which months they will be. The rest of the year sales are relatively the same. Our goal is to reach $400,000 in sales a year. That equates to $33,334.00 each month on the average. This means expanding our market by 15% while maintaining our current market. An annual increase of 15% can cause a cash flow challenge. 8% to

10% should be an annual goal. That means our goal is over a multi-year plan. Small adjustments need to be continuously made. PLAN TO SUCCEED!

- Location
  - Business Type
    - Employment
      - Hours of Operation
        - license
        - Bond

- Signage
  - Parking
    - Security
      - Product

STATUTES/ LAWS

Chapter 9   Statutes/Laws

Different locations have different laws. Don't learn the laws! PREPARE TO FAIL!

Federal laws are the same in every state. State laws vary by state. Local (City, county, township, tax district) vary by each locality. Building codes may apply to both new and existing structures. Residential locations may not allow business activity or may allow a home business. Commercial locations may or may not allow residential options. An example would be Commercial business on the street level and living spaces on the levels above or behind.

It is harmful to the health of a business to secure a location for your business, get a long-term lease and find zoning ordinances do not permit the intended use. This can be in a commercial zone that restricts certain commercial businesses. It can be in a mixed-use zoning that does not permit certain types of businesses. It can be in a residential area that may or may not allow a home-based business.

Statutes can change while you are considering a location. Check on current proposals before proceeding. It takes a period of time for most statutes to get on the books so one in the process may have been in the process for several months. Even one in consideration in the past week may pass with an effective date earlier than the date it is passed. You need to know what is intended and how it will affect you.

The help of a real estate attorney (they prefer being called "attorney") is highly recommended! Check out the statutes and ordinances applying to the location before locking it in. PLAN TO SUCCEED!

Contracts
Business disruptions
Employee limitations

RENT Lease Employees Supplier

CUSTOMERS

STRIKE   UNFAIR

UNIONS

Chapter 10   Unions

Unions don't affect your business. You have the right to set working conditions, hours and benefits that are legal. PREPARE TO FAIL!

The fact remains that some states and local laws require a "closed shop" which requires all employees to be Union members. You must follow Union rules and guidelines there.   If you have union employees you will work for the union! The definition of a "Fair Wage" is different depending on your viewpoint. A business owner must be fair while staying within budget. The business must produce enough income to pay the bills and a fair wage. It also must make a profit. Some believe a "fair wage" is the amount the employee wants or needs without respect to their ability to produce that income for the employer. A union employee may also be restricted from any activity beyond the specific job definition. This restricts the ability to "fill in" where needed outside the specific job description.

An employee was fired for changing a light bulb that had needed changed for several days. The activity was outside his job description. He needed the light to do his job but the person designated to change light bulbs hadn't got the job done for several days. The business had to reserve that job for the one with the job description.

An employee was fired for stopping to answer a question and help another worker before he logged in. He was on the way to clock in when asked and stopped to answer.

In this case he was keeping his job description but simply hadn't clocked in. Union rules are specific and protect the employee from abuses. They also protect the employee from being efficient in many cases. Each job description should include the ability to produce beyond a limited set of rules. Know your options and set a fair (to all sides) wage. PLAN TO SUCCEED!

When you do work for a government agency be prepared to pay your employees (including yourself) union wages and benefits. This may be twice what your normal wages are. While the government will try to get the lowest bid, they require the highest wages be paid. Look before you leap! You may end up losing money on a government job. In addition to the wage scale, you may find out at the pre-work meeting that there are undisclosed requirements. I had the contract to replace drapery rods and draperies, a one-man job I could do myself. I bid this as such. After I was awarded the contract, I was informed that I was required to pay someone over $22.00 an hour (wages and benefits) to watch me work as a "safety" requirement. It was pointed out I could have a heart attack on the job and no one would know. This was an estimated need of 75 hours being watched, or an additional $1650.   PLAN TO SUCCEED!

    If your business is not unionized you still need to know how union activity affects your business. Another business which uses employees with the same or similar skills as your business will have a higher wage schedule. In order to compete for good employees, you may need to match union wages. Keep this in mind when doing your business plan. Are your sales going to support the higher wages and benefits? Will this encourage employees to produce enough to earn the higher wages and benefits? PLAN TO SUCCEED!

CONTRACTS
 Pay scale
  Safety equipment
   Business Type

Chapter 11   Legal

You have checked the laws and are in compliance. The legal challenges are taken care of! PREPARE TO FAIL!

The property you do business in can have stipulations. The Landlord can have stipulations when you lease. The business district can have covenants put in place by the local businesses and enforced by the city or county. Your mortgage if you purchase real estate, or your lease if you rent can be a minefield. Have legal documents checked before signing. PLAN TO SUCCEED!

I was induced to join a company that provided training. I trusted the guarantee that was voiced. My employees felt that the company was not able to help them. This was partly because of the recession and partly because of regional differences. It cost me several thousand dollars to terminate the contract. Always read the contract and require a written copy before signing an agreement. PLAN TO SUCCEED!

Know the stipulations in every contract with your suppliers and bankers. An incidental violation or oversight can spell disaster. PLAN TO SUCCEED!

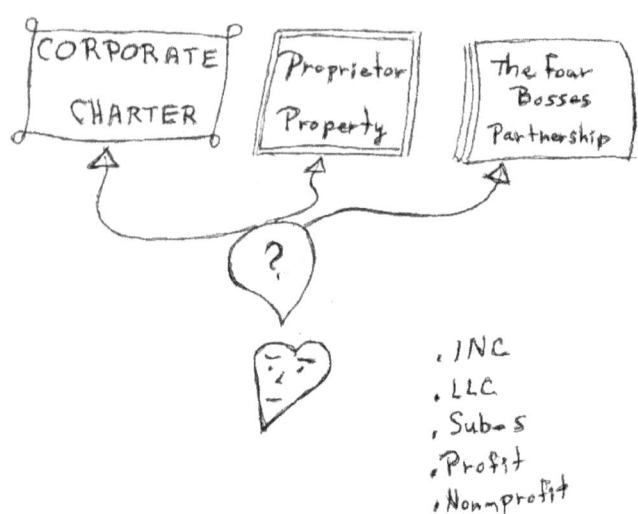

- INC
- LLC
- Sub-s
- Profit
- Nonprofit

BUSINESS TYPE

Chapter 12   Business Type

It's easier to get financing starting out with a partner. Each partner can run the business as if there were no other partner. One can run up debts without the other's knowledge. Each partner is then fully responsible for the entire debt (even if you didn't approve the debt or know about it).   PREPARE TO FAIL!

Even a partnership in marriage can go sour! A sole proprietor, Limited Liability Company, Subchapter S Corporation, a C Corporation, or a non-profit are all possibilities. Know your goals and find the best fit for your type of company. PLAN TO SUCCEED!

Three brothers were in a farming partnership. Two of the brothers actively farmed. The third brother worked off the farm and would subsidize operations at times. The third brother, in good years, put his share of the profit back into the partnership, paying income taxes from the profit of his off-farm business. One brother (actively farming) incurred debts unknown to the other two brothers. Taxes were not paid and had to be redeemed (at 12% interest) twice. The partnership was broken up along with debts and each brother assumed one third of the debts, along with one third of the assets. The partner incurring the debts ended up losing his assets. The other two worked to pay off the debts. Partnerships are financially dangerous.

In any Partnership all payments should be set up on a checking account requiring two signatures (a two-signature checking account). This allows both partners to know where the money is going. This is ideal for a two-person partnership. Where there are multiple partners setting up a trust company to receive all payments and pay all bills keeps all partners honest. In this case two of the partners should be required to present signed vouchers to the trust company for all bills to be paid. PLAN TO SUCCEED!

As sole proprietor you are the business. You are the owner. You are personally responsible for all debts, successes and failures. Legal actions (valid or not) can cause you to lose your business. A small business that provided special cakes was taken to court for not being willing to make a cake (participate in) for a wedding that was against his religious beliefs. The Constitution specifically guarantees his right to his religious beliefs, yet, he was charged with discrimination and taken to court. He lost his business. Sole proprietor type of business is open to risk. Courts do not always judge based on individual rights, statutes, or the Constitution. PLAN TO SUCCEED!

A LLC (Limited Liability Company) can be solely owned and limits the personal risk of legal actions. Small businesses should consider this in setting up the business type.

Direct Marketing happens where you offer a product directly to the consumer, personally. Businesses that offer opportunities in direct marketing have been Shakley, Amway, Mary Kay, Scentsy, Avon, Stanley, Herbalife, Tupperware, Watkins, Re-Liv, Amsoil, etc. The cost of getting into these varies. The profit from sales also varies. The requirement to purchase a certain amount of product or samples also varies. These business opportunities offer you the opportunity to develop a business with little overhead. They also require commitment to work and to produce. Your success will depend on your ability to grow your business and sales. A good home-based business is fair to you. It allows you to grow your business through personal sales and by "sponsoring" others to grow their business the way you do. You are then paid a percentage for helping them succeed. An advantage for this type of business is that you are not generally restricted geographically. Another advantage is that you are not dependent on someone else to succeed.

The key to success begins with customers, products, and service. One example given for success in direct marketing is to help customers with $7,000 of sales a month.

That would allow a possible Gross profit of $2,100.00 a month. After taxes and expenses family income would be around $1,400.00 per month. This is reduced by insurance, mortgage (or rent) payments, utility costs, and transportation (delivering the products). This isn't an easy business but it can grow. Fifty customers purchasing $140.00 a month of product each month would meet this basic goal. This means marketing something that is consumable and needed on a daily basis. IT also means finding customers who need, want, and can afford what you are offering. It means learning to service your customers.

Edna kept a 3 X 5 card file. It kept information on her customers along with the products used and the amount of time it took to use up the product. Several days before the customer ran out Edna called and asked if the customer was ready to order. This took the load off the customer trying to remember to re-order and increased customer satisfaction. The customers knew Edna cared about them.

After you max out on the number of customers you can personally serve you can sponsor (mentor) and train others to do the same. This is termed a multi-level marketing system. Helping them succeed allows you to be paid a commission on their sales. Your income grows as their success grows. However, if you don't grow your business and simply sponsor others in hopes of big rewards it is possible, they will surpass you in sales and income. These are <u>not</u> a pyramid type system (where you are always at the top, no matter what). They are businesses that need work and education to succeed. This is simply a business plan. Look at each one you help into the business as another employee. They are paid directly and you receive reward for your overhead (training, consulting, and helping them succeed). The more persons you sponsor (the more employees you would have in a business) the more customers you can serve. When they work at a "supervisor" level and sponsor others your business continues to grow. Whether you are considering having an employee or sponsoring someone into a business, you will need to train for success.

This means knowing your product(s) and your customer. It means helping others succeed so you can be successful. The first step in both types is to maximize your ability first.

A successful example of a multi-level marketing business happens when every level works as an independent business. This means finding customers (who are not sponsored) who purchase products. A good goal is to build a personal business to the point that commission income pays your basic bills. An example would be: Average sales of $200.00 per month per customer might allow a profit of $60.00. In order to have an annual income of $20,000.00 you will need 28 regular customers. Since every customer will not purchase every month, your goal would be closer to 40 regular customers. That means you would take care of 10 a week or 2 a day (five-day week). In order to help others succeed you have time to sponsor and train others to do likewise. Multi-level marketers generally pay you a bonus based on the success of those you help succeed. If this sounds easy you need to know that finding customers and servicing customers is never easy. The pay is in proportion to the success in meeting the challenge. PLAN TO SUCCEED!

A corporation issues stock to the stockholders. When there are more involved in the business a corporation sometimes makes sense. Officers are elected and Directors are chosen. They run the business and aren't required to be stockholders. The Stockholders may or may not be active in the business.

They provide the cash in the form of purchasing stock, to begin, operate, and expand the business. They receive dividends when there is a profit and the dividends are declared by the Directors. When there is no profit there are no dividends. When the value of the corporation falls the value of the stock falls. If this is lasting over a period of months the stockholders will want to sell. If the corporation needs to "redeem" the stock the corporation will fail. PLAN TO SUCCEED!

Personally, I have been a sole proprietor. I have been a LLC. I have been a stockholder in a close corporation (all stockholders are family members). I have been in a partnership.

The partnership was dissolved in order for the partners to survive. The corporation lost most of the assets when the minority stockholders chose to leave and required the corporation to pay up. At the same time the railroads refused to ship, causing unnecessary costs that diluted the corporation assets. That corporation has been reduced to three stockholders from around fifteen. I am in a multi-level marketing taking care of three customers. I haven't taken the time to grow that business. In all cases, PLAN TO SUCCEED!

We covered employee needs and the need for a good employee. Businesses are closing their doors as the owner retires and no one is trained or wanting to take over the business. Finding a business that is anchored in the community and needs a person to take over the business in a few years is ideal. You can work as an employee and learn the particulars of that business and what has made it successful. Willingness to continue the business and take care of the customers and employees will give you an opportunity to succeed without the initial debt.

There are many ways to ease transition of business ownership. Some are easier than others. The key remains, the purchase price will be paid to the previous owner in some fashion and should be insured when possible. PLAN TO SUCCEED

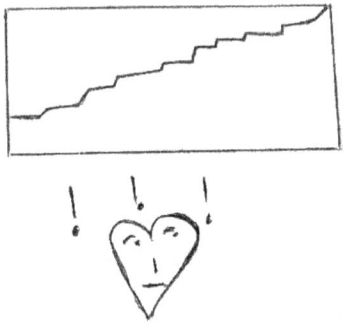

Electricity   Water
   Gas   sewer
       trash   cleaning

UTILITIES

Chapter 13   Utilities

These are easy to overlook. After all they are a small expense. A rise in utility expenses can easily drive-up expenses. This can happen with a raise in rates or a raise in usage. PREPARE TO FAIL!

Utilities, (Gas, electricity. Sewer, trash, water) vary by season and activity. They are hard to define on a monthly basis although you do have some control over them. Control your usage and watch your rates carefully. PLAN TO SUCCEED!

In the winter, in cold climates, each degree rise in heating raises the usage disproportionately. Keeping the temperature lower saves expenses. In the summer, air conditioning can get expensive. Each degree lower raises your costs disproportionately. If the business is unoccupied at night is saves money to adjust the thermostat down in the winter and up in the summer. A 6-degree adjustment for twelve hours helps balance the costs.

Heating areas that do not need the heat adds costs to the bottom line. Items that need to be kept from freezing can be kept at 50 degrees and save costs. Areas that need heat only occasionally can be left without heat until needed. Having said that, buildings do not do well with no heat in the winter and no cooling in the summer. Know your facility and handle accordingly.

When you have a choice of sources (wood, gas, electricity, solar) you may be able to reduce costs and provide the needed heat/Air conditioning necessary. PLAN TO SUCCEED!

Watch your utility costs and PLAN TO SUCCEED!

Along with the utility costs, the upkeep of the HVAC system needs to be considered. Replacing old furnace or air conditioner can be costly. PLAN TO SUCCEED!

Product   Repair
Install   Deliver
    Replace

Chapter 14   Service

Once a customer has purchased the job is done. PREPARE TO FAIL!

Repeat customers are less expensive than to find new customers. Satisfied customers are less expensive advertising for your success! Word of mouth and referrals will help you succeed. Take care of your customer! PLAN TO SUCCEED!

It's not all about MONEY! Years ago, a baker would sell a dozen donuts and include 13. This became known as a baker's dozen. This increased sales and made the baker more successful.

It's that little extra in every business that can make any business succeed. It may be a nice greeting when entering the establishment. It may be a special wrapping or extra effort to find that special item. It may mean a special order and quick delivery. It may mean low or no cost service appointment. It may mean standard rates evenings and weekends. It may mean sending a potential customer elsewhere. PLAN TO SUCCEED!

When a customer of your competitor contacts you for service on the competitor's product, how are you going to respond? If the product has a warranty your service will not be covered under the warranty.

As long as the customer understands that, you may choose to provide service at your regular price. You may choose to provide at a higher price where the service is out of normal for you. You may choose not to provide service. Keep in mind that your choice will affect your business. PLAN TO SUCCEED!

Find your "extra" and focus on delivering this low or no cost benefit. PLAN TO SUCCEED!

Our main business of window coverings includes consultation, measuring, ordering, installing, and servicing. Our consultations and measuring are free. Installing for a home when we provide the products is a set price per order. It is the same price for one window or thirty windows with the exception of shutters. We charge a per panel price for shutters. Some others charge by the square feet for shutters and by the width or by the bracket for installing other products. Added charges for installing into concrete, metal, and hollow walls are common. We haven't adopted these charges. Our customers pay for expensive products. We provide service to help them acquire these products. We are able to do this as we do all of the steps ourselves. Profit on the product allows us to keep the cost of consultations and installations down. This leads to more satisfied customers and better word of mouth. PLAN TO SUCCEED!

How good is the warranty on your products? Does your supplier honor the warranty? Do you go the extra mile to honor the warranty?

We offer a lifetime warranty with one on the suppliers we use. This warranty is extended to repairs on most of that company's products purchased from us. We don't charge to repair and only pass on a charge on any parts we pay for. This builds trust and the word-of-mouth advertising is inexpensive. PLAN TO SUCCEED!

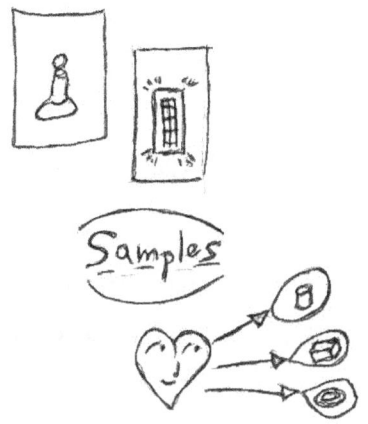

Chapter 15   Samples

If you have displays don't plan for them! PREPARE TO FAIL!

Display cabinets and display samples are expensive. They have a specific life and need to be replaced. New items need to be added. Find out what you will need and get an estimate of the cost. Find out the life expectancy of displays, are they seasonal or are they going to be valid for an extended time period (possibly several years). PLAN TO SUCCEED!

"I want one just like that!" can lead to a dissatisfied customer. The goal of service is to bring a product and customer together in a way the customer is happy. When a customer has found "the ideal solution" and you can't deliver, the sale is lost. It is hard for most customers to switch mid-stream once a decision has been made.

Keep samples current as much as possible. You may run into situations where your supplier hasn't notified you of a discontinued item. Knowing this it is good to have the customer pick two alternate options in case the first choice is discontinued. This makes the transition to an alternate item easier and a kept customer.

Touch, feel, see, hear, are your helpers in making the sale. Your customer wants to FEEL comfortable with her decision. Samples are needed to provide the experience a customer needs. PLAN TO SUCCEED!

We pay several thousand dollars a year to replace, upgrade, or add new samples each year. With this in mind, we need the profit to afford them. PLAN TO SUCCEED!

If you choose a multi-level marketing plan keep your samples fresh. Choose a business that does not require you to purchase samples you don't need or want. PLAN TO SUCCEED

Use your products, as much as possible, in your home. Test them. Try to find more uses for them! The more you know about the product and the better you understand your customer's needs, the better chance you have to succeed. PLAN TO SUCCEED!

Find us at

STREET
CITY
STATE
T.V.
Radio
SEO
e-mail

Facebook
Newspaper
Magazines
Home Show
Phone Number
Google

ADVERTISING

Chapter 16   Advertising

Who needs advertising? Those who need my services will find me! PREPARE TO FAIL!

Going fishing without equipment will catch nothing. Advertising is casting a line out with information in a way that those needing you find you easily. There are many avenues of advertising. SOC is popular. The medium you use will target a certain audience. Know your audience and find the medium that that audience sees or listens to.

A customer sees your advertising six times before seeing you. It is more efficient if the customer sees and hears your advertisement in several places. The impact is stronger.   PLAN TO SUCCEED

Who says sloppy advertising doesn't work? Actually, it doesn't! However, different styles do attract notice. If a customer doesn't see your advertising, it isn't working.

We advertise regularly with a four-piece puzzle. It stands out! We keep being asked why we don't advertise! We also use a piece developed by our supplier. It is professional and eye catching. Why don't our customers see it? Maybe it looks the same as so many others and they just glance over it! A piece that is really different catches the eye and draws customers to wonder what it is all about. The advertising needs to have an action associated with it. "We have fish for sale" doesn't trigger action. "Our fresh inventory of fish will be available for three days!" triggers " buy it soon or loose the opportunity!" PLAN TO SUCCEED!

A tornado went through town a few years ago. We developed a special postcard to mail to all those affected by the tornado. We had half a dozen responses. The piece offered a deep discount to help recovery. Why more victims didn't respond is a question. Some never received the card in the mail. Advertising will attract a percentage of those who see it. PLAN TO SUCCEED!

YEAR	1	5	10
Sales			
Expenses			
Profits			

Plan & Track
|

BUSINESS PLAN →

Chapter 17   Business Plan

Who needs a plan? They are never accurate anyway! PREPARE TO FAIL!

A business plan will never accurately specify how the business will run or costs will be. Its purpose is to have a basic plan that sets goals and brings realism into the process. The better you accurately predict costs, the better your chances of success. Besides that, any lender will require one to see if you have been realistic. More businesses fail because of inadequate funding than excess funding. A loan officer does not promote excess funding so the amount financed must be reasonable (within 10% of expected costs). PLAN TO SUCCEED!

There are two sides to a business plan. First, it accurately (as accurately as possible) projects costs and income for the business. This gives you a step by step, month by month, guideline to see if you are succeeding or need to do something different to succeed. Yes, this is a monthly projection for five years. That's sixty months! These are "goals". They are the best idea you can conceive of how successful the business can be. Once developed, this is a "living document".

This means you need to be ready to make adjustments on a daily and monthly basis to succeed.

Second, this is a document that the loan officer, or accountant, can look at to determine if you have properly planned to succeed.

When I purchased Drapery World the first bank simply told me they specialized in residential loans and did not have the expertise to evaluate my business plan. I found a bank that had the experience and the ability to suggest fine tuning to help me be successful. I calculated six sales a month would keep the bills paid. Although the amount of each sale differed, the average of previous sales would be sufficient to keep the bills paid.

My initial goal was to focus on six sales a month. After several successful months I raised the goal to ten sales a month, then twelve, then fifteen. After ten years the monthly sales vary between six and fifteen per month. We average twelve sales per month over the year. We still plan on six sales a month being able to keep the bills paid. This means keeping costs within the profit from six sales. When the sales (rarely) dip below six the income from those in excess of six allow us to pay the bills. Each new employee must be able to produce six sales a month in order to cover our cost of the employee. Although our six-sales cover rent, utilities, displays, and personal income, additional expenses for insurance and benefits are incurred for each additional employee. Also, the lost sales time when training additional employees needs to be calculated. Know your bottom limit and stay profitable. PLAN TO SUCCEED!

Caution: If you succeed beyond your projections for any month, spend only what you need to continue your success. Position yourself for a decline in sales. This means building savings while paying off debt faster where possible. This will build your credit score and make your lender happier with you. PLAN TO SUCCEED

Plan in the beginning to fail! If you don't succeed make a commitment that bankruptcy is NOT an OPTION! If the business does not succeed plan, in the beginning, how to pay off debts and bills. Build credit for the next try. PLAN TO SUCCEED!

Success depends on profit. You need cash to pay bills, employees, taxes, rent or mortgage, insurance, etc.

1) Forecast sales based on:
    - Past experience
    - Current trends
    - Industry averages
    - Seasonal variations
    - Promotion or expansion Plans
    - Available resources
    - Economic challenges
    - Government controls

2) Forecast costs based on:
    - Relationship to sales
    - Fixed Costs – uncontrollable
    - Choice- controllable costs
    - Industry averages
    - supply chain disturbances

3) Justify financial plans:
    - Determine capitalization required
    - Loan repayment-when and how much
    - Impact of interest rates and terms of loans

- Predict cash shortages
- Forecast borrowing needs
- Buy or lease comparisons
- Timing of capital purchases
- Decide when to invest idle cash
- How much in emergency fund?

4) Make management decisions:
   - Viability of new venture
   - Viability of ongoing venture
   - When to expand or contract the business
   - Expand with internally generated cash
   - When to leverage assets
   - When to raise or lower prices
   - How to add value to employees

Business influences:
1) How much or how little initial cash is available (initial capitalization)
2) How slowly bills are paid (trade credit)
3) How quickly merchandize is received, and sold
4) What price the merchandize is sold
5) How many cash/credit cards sales are made and how much/little credit is extended

6) How quickly credit accounts are collected
7) How much cash is taken out of the business

Summary of cash flows:

- Inflows
- Owner's investment
- Creditor's Debt
- Stockholder's equity
- Cash Sales
- Received on Account
- Sales of Assets
  Retirement

Outflows
Fixed Asset Purchase
Inventory Purchase
Operating expense
Owner's Draw
    Taxes
    Debt

Additional Opportunities or problems:

Inflows	Outflows
-Capital Gains	Poor Buying
-Price increases	Investment of cash
-Increased productivity	Spoilage – Theft
-Speculation	Change in tax policy
-Innovation	Change in tax rate
-Creative Marketing	Excess Repairs – lost tools
-Good Management	Bad Management
-Good Luck	Bad Luck
-Productive Employees	Non-productive employees

-

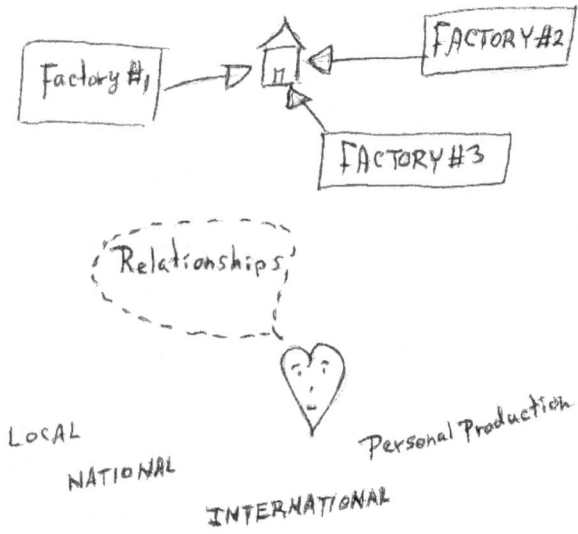

SUPPLIERS

Chapter 18   Product source(s)

Figure this out after you are in business. The sources are there! PREPARE TO FAIL!

Who are you going to purchase products from? You will need credit with them if you don't pay up front. Your business plan needs to include the cost of a "basic load" of product. This may be the products you expect to sell in a month, or two months, or a year. Remember that the products you sell must be replaced so the profit on the basic load needs to be enough to replace the basic load (at a possible higher cost), and each product sold after that needs to be able to replace itself. In addition, the profit must cover your overhead (utilities, rent, etc.), salaries, and taxes.

After establishing credit, you can ask for credit terms and pay as products are sold. This should be available after you have been in business three years. Most start-up businesses fail in the first three years.   PLAN TO SUCCEED!

In a start-up business, most suppliers will require pre-payment for your products. This means you will need to receive a down payment, up front, large enough to pay for the product upon order.

After you establish credit (six months to a year) you can request a thirty-day account. Your bill is normally due thirty days from the date the product is shipped to you. This gives you some breathing room. Make sure the supplier receives the payment by the due date! PLAN TO SUCCEED!

Wayne purchased an old filling station. He was determined to demolish the building and build a nice convenience store. He researched information on existing stores, product suppliers, traffic movement at that location (corner of two highways), cost of getting blueprints and construction, all before he went for the loan. His store was successful. For security (24 hours a day) he always had two employees present and they were instructed never to be together. One was always able to call for police without being noticed. This avoided robberies. PLAN TO SUCCEED!

We see the prices of gasoline rise and fall with the season, weather, and oil prices. If you have a service station (selling fuel) you need to plan for additional purchase prices when your price increases to replace the fuel you sell. The profit margin for gasoline is normally three to five cents per gallon. The rest of the price goes to electricity, taxes, shipping, refining, and the price of oil. A five-cent increase in your cost can cause a financial crisis if not planned for. PLAN TO SUCCEED!

Products can make or break you! Are they manufactured in this country? What is the quality? What service does the manufacturer provide? What is the warranty? Do they back the warranty? Does the product fit (quality and price) your ideal customer base? How much help do you get from the supplier in promoting their products? Is the company well established? How are they doing financially? You need to learn as much about your supplier as they learn about you! PLAN TO SUCCEED!

This is an advantage of purchasing a "going concern", a business that is alive and successful. The supply chain is already established. With proper transitions the suppliers can be kept and the business relationships can be continued. Instead of searching for suppliers you can focus on developing a relationship with existing suppliers. PLAN TO SUCCEED!

MORTGAGE   BUSINESS LOAN

HOME LOAN

CONSTRUCTION LOAN

REVOLVING LOAN

SELF BANKING

BUDGET PLANNING

Chapter 19   Banking

What difference does it make? Any bank will do! PREPARE TO FAIL!

The terms of borrowing, the type of checking account, savings account, and construction mortgage, can break you faster than you can get started. A bank that does business in the type of industry you are in is a good place to start. Find out where your competition banks are and start there. Find a bank that you can have a personal relationship with. PLAN TO SUCCEED!

Wayne worked on commission and saved for the down times. 1957 was a down year. The draught prevented crops from producing. The Bank called Wayne in and informed him they were foreclosing on a mortgage. He told them they couldn't as he had not missed a payment. They informed him that they had determined that he would not be able to make a payment in the future and were proceeding to foreclose. Wayne walked to the bank across the street, withdrew savings, walked back across the street, and paid the mortgage off. That bank lost his business. It also made it hard on his family as the children had outgrown their shoes and could not have new shoes that year. Save for the down times! PLAN TO SUCCEED!

A note mentioned earlier should be repeated. Find a bank that knows your type of business and has expertise to guide you to be more successful. PLAN TO SUCCEED!

Other options are credit unions, savings and loans, and angel investors. Each has strengths and weaknesses. Your business plan and the fit of your type of business to the institution will be a deciding factor. PLAN TO SUCCEED!

Your credit has a lot to do with your relationship with any financial institution. Starting out you may need to work for several years establishing credit. The key- PAY YOUR BILLS ON TIME. This means planning to have the payment to the supplier (including utilities and landlord) at least a day before the payment is due. Plan for delays in the mail. Make sure the money is available to make the payments on time without having an overdraft. Then, find good terms for a revolving loan. This is a loan and costs interest for the amount drawn at any time. The loan amount can fluctuate from zero to the maximum established for the loan. It allows you to capture opportunities that you might otherwise miss. The goal is to keep the loan low or zero and only use it for an occasional larger order that you can pay off soon. PLAN TO SUCCEED!

Keep in mind that financial institutions have bills to pay. They are in the business to make a profit. Keeping your bills paid on time will reduce their paperwork and reduce their operating costs.

When dealing with a financial institution find one that offers good terms and service for you. Find one that will help you succeed both financially and with a good business plan. PLAN TO SUCCEED

I had a new customer who needed to have shutters and blinds installed prior to closing on a house. This required me to carry the cost for a couple of months as I needed to pay for the product before closing. The customer wrapped the cost into his mortgage and the money wasn't available until closing. Our revolving loan made this sale possible. If we had used the maximum limit on the loan this sale wouldn't have been possible. The customer informed me the competition didn't have the ability to finance the project. PLAN TO SUCCEED!

Stay away from keeping a budget. PLAN TO FAIL!

Knowing your income and expenses on a weekly, monthly, quarterly, annual basis, you PLAN TO SUCCEED!

First priority: Pay your suppliers!

Second priority: Pay on your debt!

Third priority: Pay your taxes!

Fourth priority: Feed the cow! To produce you need a healthy animal. If you ant milk you feed the cow. If you want a healthy business you need to provide advertising, pay employees, and keep a viable web site.

Fifth priority: Pay utilities. And put some into savings.

There are two methods to increase finances: Personal labor, and money working at interest (savings, investments, reduced cost of debt). Focus on these from the beginning and you PLAN TO SUCCEED!

- INDIVIDUALS
- COMPANIES
- PRODUCERS
- CONSUMERS

CUSTOMERS

Chapter 20   Customers

Who needs to be concerned about customers? PREPARE TO FAIL!

The lubrication that keeps a business going is the customer. The customer pays the bills. The customer pays the salaries. A happy customer promotes your business. An unhappy customer will tell seven people how bad you are. That's like putting sand in your fuel tank.

Who is your customer? What age range uses your product? If you can't define an age range then look at household income, location, lifestyles, needs, and desires. Then, find ways to reach your potential customers so that they can find you. Put your major effort into the ideal customer. Meanwhile don't overlook customers that don't fit the ideal. Be open to going beyond the fence, above the wall, through the thicket, on the other side, and below the curve. Focus on customer service and PLAN TO SUCCEED!

Our primary customer base is the old home/ new home owner. This is a residential market. The other side of the fence would be commercial facilities. Above the wall would be new homes/ new home owners. Through the thicket would be contracts that we need to bid. These take a lot of time to bid and can end without business. Below the curve would be the entry market, lower income, less expensive products, and less profit. Although we would like to make every sale at the top it's the small sales that pay the bills. There are more of them. PLAN TO SUCCEED!

When a customer needs one window covered, we work to provide the service. When a customer needs repairs, we work to provide the service. When a customer needs windows covered in an office or commercial building, we work to provide the service. When a customer needs an "entry level" product to keep the cost affordable, we work to provide the service. Our focus in on service over profit. There are times it costs us to provide service. If done properly, this is inexpensive advertising. PLAN TO SUCCEED!

To be successful we stopped selling products and sell solutions. We sell service! We sell solutions to situations our customers have encountered. We PLAN TO SUCCEED!

SALES

Chapter 21 Sales

There will be enough sales to pay the bills. I don't need to worry about them! PREPARE TO FAIL!

What will your average sale be? How much profit is in that sale? How many of those do you need each week, or each month, or each year to pay the bills? This is your Base Acceptable Bottom. It's just enough to survive! It's the NECESSARY production to survive! Exceeding that brings profit for your income and the company growth. PLAN TO SUCCEED!

When I purchased Drapery World in 1999, I calculated I needed 6 sales a month to pay the rent, utilities, and overhead expenses. The seventh sale gave me income for the family. My goal was to never drop below 6 and to shoot for 10 sales a month. Years later the goal was raised to 12 a month. Very few months have dropped below 6 and some months have exceeded 12. Annual sales should increase no more than 10% a year or finances get out of whack. We increased 20% per year for several years, working 60 to 80 hours a week. It became more difficult to keep up with paying bills. The bank increased our line of credit as we got larger orders. It's the weekly and monthly goals that are the foundation for growth and success. PLAN TO SUCCEED!

Milk the cow! A dairy farmer succeeds by producing milk. The cows need to produce in order for the farmer to succeed. In order for the cows to produce they must be fed. Your business must operate the same way.

It must produce for you to succeed. You must feed the business in order for it to produce. That means marketing, facilities, utilities, personnel, payroll, tools, vehicles, etc. Feed to cow before feeding yourself or your business will fail! Feed the business improperly and you will not have enough produce to pay the bills! If the dairy farmer fed wheat to the cows they would founder and be lost. Wheat is good for cattle…in small amounts, mixed with the proper feed. In order to milk the cow, she must be fed. In order for the business to produce it must be fed properly. PLAN TO SUCCEED!

"PAY YOURSELF FIRST!" This is one of the best slogans in successful business. It is also one of the most misunderstood slogans that can lead to quick failure. ALWAYS pay your bills first! ALWAYS pay your utilities and taxes first! After all bills, salaries, benefits interest, mortgage/rent and insurance are paid you may have enough left over for a salary. The idea is to set aside <u>a portion of your salary</u> <u>or commission</u> every pay day into some sort of retirement account before you spend the rest (home mortgage/rent, utilities, food, clothing, education, vehicle expenses, medical expenses, etc.). PLAN TO SUCCEED!

- High traffic area
- Low rent area
- Accessability

LOCATION

Chapter 22   Location

It doesn't matter as long as people can find me!
PREPARE TO FAIL!

Location, Location, Location, the three important qualities of real estate. This is true of a home and it is true also of a business. A visible, well kept up, location at a reasonable price is ideal. Even an ideal place needs to be affordable and have a reasonable landlord.

We were offered a prime location several years ago. The facility is on a busy street with thousands of cars passing daily. The purchase price was $300,000 for a "shell". Then the interior needed finished (say another $100,000), we chose to relocate to a downtown location with rent much lower than our mortgage would be at that location. The current location is good and also affordable. The space was "move in" ready. When planning location, it must be affordable! PLAN TO SUCCEED!

> When deciding on a location you need to find answers to some questions:
> - Is the space affordable?

- Is the space adequate for your business?
- Who is responsible for upkeep?
- Who is responsible for taxes?
- What visibility will the location give you?
- Is the visibility good for the customers you need to reach?

Although we located downtown, we have few "walk ins". Most of our customers are referrals from previous customers, return business from prior customers, or customers who found advertising and called for service. We suggest they first come into our showroom and experience the products on display. We note which products they need, like, and (hopefully) can afford. Then, we schedule a free home consultation to take sample books to the home (or office). At this time, we measure, choose patterns and colors, and provide a quote for doing the job.

We are in a location where parking is a challenge. Still, it is seen as a good location by being "down town". PLAN TO SUCCEED!

There are three important factors in determining location. Will the location help you be successful? How will your customers find you? Does your product fir the location?

So how do you answer the important factors? Survey, survey, survey! Ask potential customers if they will use you at that location? Have a professional surveyor determine if the traffic count, the local businesses, and the product you are selling all come together. PLAN TO SUCCEED!

♥

〔 REMEMBER ME 〕

| LOGO |

Chapter 23   Logo

You don't need a logo starting out! PREPARE TO FAIL!

Branding is big. People will not remember your name as well as the well-designed logo. The logo must tell a story in picture format. Does it show integrity, identity, and focus? Is it remember able? When a potential customer needs your service will they remember your logo, slogan, or service?

The human mind remembers pictures longer than words. A good logo is a picture that describes your business in a way that can be remembered.

A logo says "permanent". It tells the customer you are in business to stay!   PLAN TO SUCCEED!

Our logo is a four-pane window with a letter in each pane (D, W, A, B). Our business covers and dresses windows. Our business name is <u>D</u>rapery <u>W</u>orld <u>and</u> <u>B</u>linds. The logo is our business! PLAN TO SUCCEED!

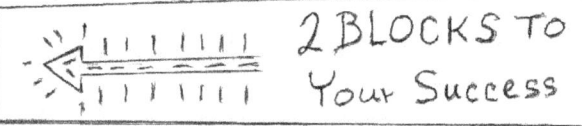

SIGNAGE

Chapter 24   Signage

I don't need a sign. Advertising my address will bring customers to me! PREPARE TO FAIL!

Did you ever go to a location and feel you were in the wrong place because it looked that they were out of business? Customers can literally be at your front door and not come in because they think they are at the wrong place. Signs that are seen easily and let customers know "This is where we are" are necessary. We moved locations in 2005. The previous location was out of the way and hard to find. The new location was on Main Street. We almost went out of business. People walked by thinking we were a closed business. Ads in the newspaper telling of the move weren't noticed. The city did not approve a sign permit. After five months we got a lighted sign in the window which did not require a permit. We survived on bank loans. It took years to pay back those loans while paying regular expenses. I didn't know I could have an inside lighted sign when we moved. I didn't know a sign permit for a sign on the outside of the building would be so hard to acquire. The lighted sign helped stay in business. Years later we were able to get outside signs. The original cost of $3,000 ended up to cost $23,000 for the outside signs. PLAN TO SUCCEED!

There are signs for a building. There are yard signs (like those realtors use). There are vehicle signs (both magnetic and a "wrap"). There are uniforms and hats. There are hand-outs (pens, bags, etc.). All of these are ways of promoting your business with signs. Pick the ones that best promote your business and are affordable. PLAN TO SUCCEED!

(tm)

| Trade Mark |

Chapter 25   Trademark and Patent

You don't need a trademark! No one will want to duplicate your idea! PREPARE TO FAIL!

There are businesses that do nothing but take original plans and make the product cheaper. They have little advertising costs as you have advertised the usefulness and effectiveness of the product. They only have to let people already sold on the idea that they can have a cheaper solution. If you have an original idea and don't secure it with a trademark or have a product and don't secure it with a patent you are planning to fail. PLAN TO SCUCCEED!

"It's the logical choice!", "Things go better with Pepsi", "The cool refreshing beer", "We make money the old-fashioned way…we earn it", "Route 66", "You are wanted", "We dress insides", "The blind guys help you see".

Your business name can be your trademark. Your product name can be your trademark. Having a trademark prevents competitors from using your name to confuse your customers and undercut you.

Catchy slogans can be trademarks! They are designed to put a picture in your mind that triggers a want or a need. They are successful. You need one! PLAN TO SUCCEED!

New Ownership II
Grand Opening

New/Existing Business

Chapter 26   New/Existing

Is this a new business or an existing business? If you don't find out the market, the possible success of the business, the trend of the sales in that business you PREPARE TO FAIL!

A business, successfully sewing rank on military uniforms could be a going concern. When the military changed to Velcro attachments, ending the need to sew, the business had outlived its usefulness. If you were near an Army Post there would be a failing business. If you were near an Air Force Base the business would, currently, be successful. You need to know the market and the trends.

Purchasing an existing business? What is the sales volume? What is the profit? What are the expenses? How are these expected to change? How much of the business is "blue sky". That's the personal tie the customers have to the current owner! How much "blue sky" can you preserve? Paying full cost for a business and watching the sales drop off can lead to failure! How does the current owner maintain the current customer base? Can you emulate this? Is the current owner going to be active during the three-year transition period? In sales? Advertising? Consultant?

A new business must start with empty ledgers. There is no income. There are no customers. There are only expenses. Keeping the expenses down while attracting valued customers and good employees is a balancing act many entrepreneurs never learn to achieve. PLAN TO SUCCEED!

What is the competition? Can you offer something unique and compete in the same business as others in your market area. Plumbers may have weekend service without charging overtime to compete. How promptly can you make a service call? Is your product better, more durable, or more functional? PLAN TO SUCCEED!

A business owner sold the business with the idea "you can build it". The sales price was based on future growth. There were six competitors in the area and the sales for the business had fallen off over the previous years. The new owner bought the "business" and also rented the facility from the prior owner. This was an established business! The new owner worked the business for three years and returned it to the previous owner. The growth did not occur! Investing requires deep research. Was the business losing market share on price? Was the problem quality? Was the problem service? Was the problem location? Was the problem lack of visibility (advertising, location, signage, etc.)? Without knowing the challenges up front you cannot address them and succeed. PLAN TO SUCCEED!

    A company owned al old service station. They decided to rebuild and put a convenience store on the property. They hired a company to survey traffic flow, competition, need, etc. When this was complete, they researched building structures and store features. They successfully built a convenience store that was ideally located and properly furnished. The store was a success! PLAN TO SUCCEED!

| Experience ⟶ New Owner |

| MENTOR |

Chapter 27   Mentor

Be you own boss! Set your own hours! Work the system you have been taught! These are all good. If this is all you do you PREPARE TO FAIL!

All classes teach the basics. They don't cover the small things that can pop up and how to manage them. Each business will have situations pop up. The same type of business at different end of town, or even across the street, will have different challenges. If you don't start out working for a successful business and learn on-the-job or have a mentor you PREPARE TO FAIL!

For the first years, a salary income working for another business gives stability and on-the-job training. Taking over an existing business with a mentor allows you to get your feet on the ground and have on-the-job-training. PLAN TO SUCCEED!

What is a mentor? The person who is successful in the type of business you are going into! This person will advise ways to run the business. You can get training that school never taught. The challenge starts when your ideas of running a business are set and the mentor's advice conflicts with your ideas. Do you listen to the mentor or run it your way? For the first three years, following the advice of a mentor, you have a better chance of success. PLAN TO SUCCEED!

A mentor can be someone who is willing to have you work together. As you observe the actions, traits and successes of that person you are being "Mentored". An insurance agent would dedicate one day a month working with another insurance agent. One of the agents made money each month. The other learned and adjusted attitudes. The agents took turns lining up appointments. They took turns evaluating each other. Their productivity increased. Joint mentoring can be successful! PLAN TO SUCCEED!

When I purchased Drapery World and transitioned from an insurance agent to window treatments the previous owner agreed to stay as a (unpaid) consultant. Cell phones were still fairly new so I purchased two. I kept one and gave one to my consultant so I could get advice from the golf course if needed. He was invaluable. His lessons went like "I always count the ladders on a wood blind to determine to position of a center bracket!" There was a reason this was necessary! When he would say what he would do I learned quickly to understand "this is

the way to do the job". After a few years I made some small adjustments. The basics were learned first!
PLAN TO SUCCEED!

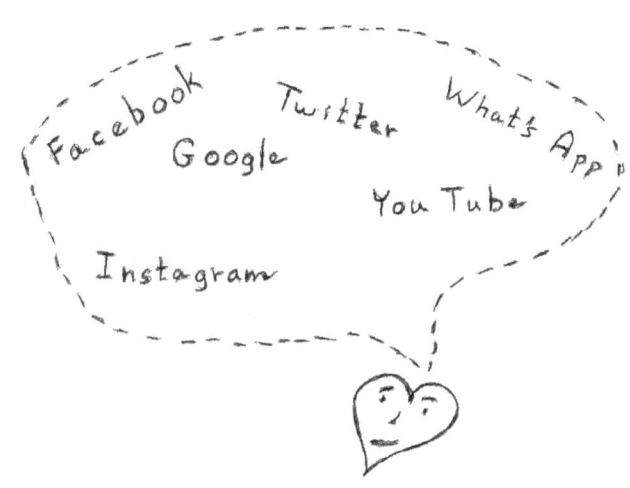

Social Media

Chapter 28   Social Media

Hide your product from the competition. Serve friends and relatives. Don't expand your area of influence…PREPARE TO FAIL!

Communication, Advertising, and Commitment are absolutely necessary for a business to succeed.

Start with friends and relatives. Who are their friends? Who are the friends' friends? Who are the….? You get the idea! Reach beyond your ability to personally meet each potential customer. Sell service! Sell Commitment to their success! Sell solutions to situations that customers need, want, or are required to have for living.

Social media has become "family". It has become the mail box where personal messages abound. You can reach more potential customers faster than in the past. Keep in mind that each new customer has had an average of 6 contacts from you (or your business) before becoming a customer. It takes 100 potential customers to yield three customers. This means of the 100 persons that see you. Three will see you an average of six times and become customers. Social Media is the best system to contact many potential customers daily.

Sell service? Are you going to sell over the internet? How are you going to service? Where is the personal touch? Selling over the internet requires narrow margins that require a larger volume of sales to provide a good income. Products that don't need serviced, that are quickly expendable or used up work fairly well here.

Customers purchasing items that need replaced regularly can be good repeat customers when you service the account and replace the items quickly when needed. Products that are durable and may need adjusting, cleaning, or repairs are better marketed in a geographical area you (or your employees) can service personally. Social media works to inform these customers of the product and local service. In this case social media acts as advertising rather than selling.

It is better to keep prices away from the social media site and market available service.

Keeping Social local! Selling at a location (store) is still a strong tie to local sales for many products. Consumers want service before and after the sale. They want to be able to see and touch the product.

Focus on letting your customers know that you provide this service. PLAN TO SUCCEED!

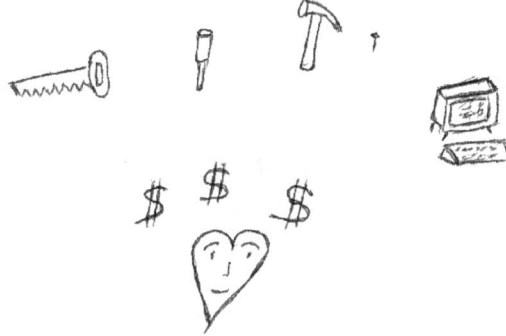

Tools

Chapter 29   Tools

Tools are replaceable. Don't worry about losing them! PREPARE TO FAIL!

Tools are expensive! Inventory them. Keep track of them. Take care of them. Reduce unnecessary costs of replacement.

Joe worked digging with a shovel each day in his job. At the end of the day, he cleaned the dirt off the shovel, dried it and oiled it. The next day it was easier to work with. Rust and dirt make digging harder. Rust and dirt will ruin a shovel. Joe saved a lot of money by not having to replace the shovel. His shovel lasted many years. Tools need to be cared for to last. PLAN TO SUCCEED

Paper for the office printer is a small item that can balloon into an expensive item. Print what is necessary and reduce paper costs. This goes for staples, file folders, note pads, pens, pencils, order pads, etc. The costs of these Office Supplies can get out of hand. The more paper you print the more ink or laser cartridges you will need. Then a shredder is needed for privacy. Control your Office Supplies and PLAN TO SUCCEED!

Computers, cell phones, tablets, and vehicles are all tools. They are expensive and will need to be replaced every few years as they wear out or become outdated. Plan to save for replacement. PLAN TO SUCCEED!

Office Supplies

Chapter 30   Office Supplies

Expendables are easy to lose track of. Pens, paper clips, paper, notebooks, note cards, post-its, stamps, credit card supplies, printer ink/ paper/laser cartridge, etc. can be handy for everything besides business. A little here and a little there adds up to a big expense. Watch your usage and keep it to necessary usage.

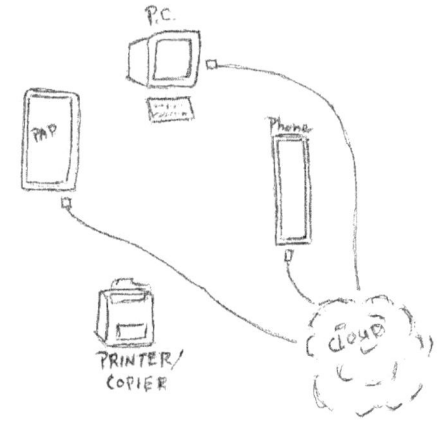

Chapter 31   Technology

Computers, phones, electronic -devices, who needs them? They just get in the way! PREPARE TO FAIL!

There are several reasons you need to add this to your business:

- Your competition is here.
- Your advertising here gets to customer's homes other media may not
- With a professional logo and web page you are seen as "in Business"
- Customers need to be able to contact you (phone, e-mail, text, etc.)
- People looking for your services or products search the internet first
- More people will find you, your location, and your contacts.

PLAN TO SUCCEED!

Did you ever call a company for a quote or service and listen to the phone ring indefinitely? Maybe you were fortunate enough to get an answering machine. If you were lucky the machine actually recorded the message. Maybe someone listened to the message sometime in the following weeks. Maybe you waited and called back. Most customers would seek out a competitor who was able to be contacted and provided service.

This applies to e-mail. More customers are looking for immediate response by e-mail. If they don't hear within a few hours, they feel neglected.

Computer software becomes obsolete in three to five years. The operating system of the computer also becomes obsolete in five to seven years. The TRS 80 belongs in a museum. Programs are bigger, more complex, take more storage, and require faster processors. Plan to replace computers and software as you grow. PLAN TO SUCCEED

ETHICS

Chapter 32   Ethics

All's fair in war and business. The competitive environment requires business to fight with whatever means necessary to succeed. PREPARE TO FAIL!

Unethical business practices will, eventually, run aground violating laws and teaching consumers not to trust your company. Ethical companies may grow slower and lose some business along the way. The customers lost will not be good customers in the long run. The long run is your goal! A good business is like a person who eats properly, exercises properly, avoids unhealthy practices, and controls stress. That business is designed to grow and succeed beyond the life of those who start the business.

Jim designed his business plan based on the grocery store model. Each week a grocery store will have sales on some store items. Those items get the customers into the store. Once there, they will purchase other items with a higher profit margin. Jim had a home service business. Consultations were free. That got him into the home to introduce his product and services. This is useful for any home service business; window cleaning, direct sales of soaps and personal items, gutters, roofing, window coverings, lawn care, internet services, phone services, etc. Then, Jim offered a competitive price for hourly wages, follow-up repairs, touch-ups, and concerns.

Offering value in both product and service allowed Jim to succeed without cutting price for the product. Jim considered the free and lower price services as a cost of advertising. Word of Mouth is the best advertising a business can promote. It all starts with happy customers who feel appreciated and not taken advantage.

A window shade manufacturer had businesses selling in box stores, on the internet, and out of store fronts. Service was a trademark. The warranty was valued. Items sold through the internet and in box stores were not able to provide the valued service. The company stopped all sales through channels that did not provide the service desired. Sales volume was reduced. Customer satisfaction increased. Window shade stores provided the required services and had increased volume. We took advantage of offered training and acquired certifications in customer service, product service, and Master Installation. PLAN TO SUCCEED!

Ethics means treating customers honestly and fairly while having enough profit to pay your bills and grow your business. PLAN TO SUCCEED!

The Golden Rule- Treat others as you would like to be treated! PLAN TO SUCCEED!

The easy sale:

The customer needs a product and either can't find it or the effort at finding it is troublesome. You have that product that fits what the customer wants, is affordable, and can more easily (your service) be acquired. When you understand what the customer needs and that you can provide that need you put the customer in the driver's seat. The next questions the customer generally asks is "how can I get it?" And, "how soon can I have it?" All you need to do is help the customer acquire it.

Profit is the available resource to pay bills and keep in business. Special deals for relatives, friends, etc. are 100% COST. An employer I knew had a special rate for anyone wanting a "deal". He charged 10% over the regular price. The additional effort to service certain customers could demand a much higher price. 10% over the regular price, for additional service, is a deal.

Thomas Deaver worked as a life and health insurance agent achieving a 96% persistency in life policies and 92% persistency in health policies. His business was based on service.

He then took an opportunity to work closer to home, purchasing a business doing $65,000 in annual sales and building it with a 20% increase in sales each year during the good years. His business was based on service.

At one time he started a business, having a product manufactured. Challenges with the manufacturing caused some products not to work. He stopped selling until the challenges were identified and corrected. His business was based on service.

Other books by Thomas Deaver:

The Stage: Finding Love

Christmas at 50

Life Insurance for Regular People

Rhyme in Time

Rhyme in Time 2

The War Years

www.ingramcontent.com/pod-product-compliance
Lightning Source LLC
Chambersburg PA
CBHW050911160426
43194CB00011B/2368